"Engaging questions of race, privilege, and culture can be uncomfortable. Jody Fernando's *Pondering Privilege* is a remarkably helpful guide, helping Christ-followers to engage with humility and grace."

Matthew Soerens
U.S. Director of Church Mobilization, World Relief
Co-author, *Welcoming the Stranger: Justice, Compassion and Truth in the Immigration Debate*

"Jody Fernando has written a thoughtful, humble, helpful, and powerful book about privilege in American society. As an African American, I have often found it difficult to discuss issues of race and power with members of the dominant culture—particularly in Christian settings. I've been dismissed, frequently considered to be simply an angry man whose concerns are not valid in this day and age. I have appreciated White allies who could speak when my voice, and that of many other African Americans, was not being heard.

Ms. Fernando's voice is not one of a self-righteous, strident cynic. Hers is the voice of a compassionate fellow traveler on a journey of discovering how to demonstrate the love of Jesus in a racialized, patriarchal, and stratified society. I am hopeful that her writing can have a huge impact on all with open hearts and minds. I enthusiastically recommend *Pondering Privilege*."

Dr. Dennis R. Edwards
Senior Pastor, Sanctuary Covenant Church
Minneapolis, Minnesota

"*Pondering Privilege* is an invitation from a White Christian to White Christians to dip their toes and then jump in to a world that isn't afraid to make mistakes and learn about racial differences and privilege.

This is an accessible book that addresses the fear of making mistakes as well as the desire to separate or distance oneself from our country's (and church's) racist histories. Jody Wiley Fernando takes personal experiences and lessons learned as an educator and practitioner and has written a guide any individual or group truly interested in understanding White privilege would benefit from."

Kathy Khang,
Co-author, *More Than Serving Tea*,
and blogger at www.kathykhang.com

"I've known Jody Wiley Fernando primarily through her words —first through her blog, then assorted Facebook exchanges, and now through this important book. Her words have been vulnerable, provocative, and challenging—but always wrapped in humility, grace, and a desire to both teach and learn.

Pondering Privilege will not be a comfortable read for anyone, but it provides a foundation for the kinds of honest conversations about race, culture, and faith that we must have (over and over) before we can ever move forward as a society and as the church."

Edward Gilbreath
Author of *Reconciliation Blues: A Black Evangelical's Inside View of White Christianity*

Pondering Privilege

Toward a Deeper Understanding of Whiteness, Race, and Faith

by Jody Wiley Fernando, M.A., M.Ed.

Printed in the United State of America First Printing, 2016
ISBN 978-0-911802-8409 NextStep Publishers 7890 12th Ave. S., Minneapolis, MN 55425 www.nsresources.com

"We need to remember that the house of God
is not limited to a building that we usually visit
for only a few hours on Sunday.
The house of God is not a safe place.
It is a cross where time and eternity meet,
and where we are
– or should be –
challenged to live more vulnerably,
more interdependently."

Madeline L'Engle

Table of Contents

Acknowledgements

This book was born out of my life's circumstances. It haphazardly made its way into existence over a period of several years, and would not have happened without the many people who have walked alongside me with vulnerability, kindness, and patience.

My husband, Rukshan, could be listed as a co-author of this book. He has walked every step of this journey (and then some!) with me, helped me process issues of race I didn't understand, called me out on my own privilege, and given me the gift of his vulnerability and unconditional love. Writers/teachers aren't exactly known for being easy to live with or willing to be taught; yet he's navigated this stubborn soul with kindhearted gentleness and gracious wisdom. Walking in partnership with him is one of the most precious and humbling gifts of my life.

Joining the entire Fernando family has been the icing on the cake of our marriage. Not all foreign wives are received into families with the warmth and kindness that the Fernando family has extended to me. They have been my spiritual teachers, modeling cultural humility and living lives of reconciliation that have put my western 'sensibilities' to shame. While their immense talents, selfless sacrifice, and committed service will never make global headlines, they deepen and broaden Christ's kingdom with a fierceness and commitment I've rarely seen in American Christianity.

I count my brother- and sister-in-law, John and Shanika, as some of the most influential people in my life. Their humble spirits and patient hearts have modeled cultural humility in ways that both challenge and inspire me to better love my neighbors. I am especially grateful to them for the feedback and editing they generously offered for this book.

My children have endured the perils of a writer-mother who sneaks away to tap the words out of her brain early mornings and any-other-chance-she-can-get. They, along with my precious nieces and nephews, inspire me to pursue making these rough racial places plain so that their lives will not tell the same stories that the past does.

In their wisdom and love, my parents held on tight as I roller-coastered through the angry spewing and accusations that arise as an understanding of racial justice develops in White minds and hearts. To their great credit, they listened and engaged my youthful passions and pondered these 'new' ideas right along with me. While many people grow set in their ways in their older years, I long to follow my parents' example of lifelong learning and growth.

There have been so many others along the way who have spoken into my understanding of racial issues. My youth pastor, Kevin, opened the door to this path by simply providing opportunities to interact with other races, challenging me to see the world beyond my backyard, and encouraging me to engage hard issues with honesty and open-mindedness. I will be forever grateful to Felicia for her patience, courage, and honesty with this once clueless White girl. She was one of the first to push open the door to my understanding. I don't know where I'd be without Lauren, my first friend in California willing to share the truth of her life with me. Her faithful friendship, awesome proofreading, and willingness to stare life straight in the eye are precious gifts to me.

It has been a joy to walk alongside my only lifelong friend, Holly Daly, from growing up in our small Indiana town to raising interracial families and navigating urban realities. She understands my story like no other. My dear friends Johanna, Sarah V., and Sarah B. have been my spiritual scaffolding—pillars who hold up my soul when my faith feels too weak to continue. And I can't help but smile every time I think of the Messers, the Warnocks, and the Lightfoots, warm porch lights who lessened the load of the isolation of the cornfields simply because they *saw* us and acknowledged the heavy burden we carried of being 'the only ones'.

Finally, I cannot forget the countless students, teachers, writers, and readers who have humbly and patiently allowed me honest glimpses into their world. Their stories linger behind every word on these pages.

Introduction

Having recently relocated to the Los Angeles area from the mono-cultural, rural cornfields of Indiana, my interracial and intercultural family spent months looking for a church to attend. One of our hopes for a new church was a bit of diversity, but even near LA, we didn't have much luck finding a multicultural church that fit.

For several months we attended one church that had minimal diversity but still had other qualities that drew us in. However, the longer we stayed, the more we felt like outsiders, and were unsure whether this was due to race or something else. We'd made friends with another person of color there and met with him and his wife to discuss their experience with the church. He affirmed our sense that we were 'outsiders', expressed he had felt the same way many times, and observed, "They're kind. They are good people. They love the Lord. They just don't know they're being White."

It was like a light bulb turned on for me. This was the reality I'd seen time and again as I observed race relations in the church. So many White people I'd known over the years were completely ignorant, not only of their race, but of the culture their skin carried with it and its impact on anyone from differing racial backgrounds. They didn't intend to exclude people unlike them; they simply had no idea how their ignorance about race and culture made them exclusionary.

I originally published *When White People Don't Know They're Being White*, the first chapter included in this study on my then-quiet blog *Between Worlds* (thelinkbetweenworlds.com). Much to my surprise, it went viral and spawned a great deal of discussion, reprints, and spin-off posts. Clearly, the idea hit a chord that people needed to discuss. Since then, the national conversation on race has only grown more polarized and divisive.

I wrote this book as part study guide, part conversation-over-coffee about the roads I have walked and lessons I have learned about privilege in society today. Much of the additional material here was originally posted on *Between Worlds* and has been adapted for personal reflection and group discussion. Each section includes questions which allow readers to spend some time pondering the information presented. It is my hope that readers might utilize it to explore their own understanding of race relations and to facilitate a cultural understanding that has not traditionally been a part of predominantly White fellowships.

1

An Appeal to Cultural Humility

The headlines told a difficult story. A prominent Christian leader made insensitive statements about a particular ethnic group. Members of that ethnic group responded with accusations of racism and requests for an apology. Confused and defensive, the leader's supporters asked how people could be so easily offended and suggested they needed thicker skin and more forgiving hearts.[1]

Whenever I hear about such conversations, I ache inside. These conversations and ignorant assumptions, the temptation to stay quiet in the face of stifling, and the belittling language associated with them are not new to me. Over the years, I have sat with many aching hearts—including those of my own family—over the racially insensitive comments or assumptions of others. While I am always grateful to hear of eventual apologies, these situations highlight an all too common occurrence between the majority and minority experience that, in my observation, most White people don't understand.

In case you're White and feeling defensive, please know that I'm White too. I hope this fact helps to lower defenses, because this study is intended specifically for White Christian leaders in the

American church. I'm concerned because I know firsthand how good-hearted and well-intentioned our actions often are, and because I know we often do not understand their harmful impact. I write as someone who has made the ignorant comment, asked the stupid question, held the racist assumption, and feared offending others by opening my mouth. I also write as the only White person in my household who, for nearly two decades now, has had the great fortune to see through others' eyes on a daily basis.

As a member of a majority ethnic group, when I grapple with issues of race and class, I am repeatedly confronted by a host of complex power dynamics. Take, for example, the power dynamics of race and gender represented in a popular Christian music video[2] in which Christians from around the world sing together in many languages. I felt conflicted after watching this video, for I could clearly see that the creators were trying to showcase the beauty of God's diverse world; but I was also uncomfortable with the persistent pattern of a White man leading the world in song along with video shots of non-Whites doing things like carrying bananas, living in slums, and standing in mud. I understood why some were quick to defend the pure intention behind the video, but I was still saddened by the clichéd images of what is sometimes called the "White savior" mentality.

This mentality is far too prevalent and accepted in the American protestant church. It is such a significant part of our narrative that we are often unaware of it. It communicates that White people are better, smarter, and more capable of holding the power. It places us as central and others as peripheral, and is reinforced by our unwillingness to face variations of formal and informal colonialism.

We didn't do it, right?

That's not our story.

My family didn't own slaves.

The historical privilege of our white skin allows us to benefit from historical power structures. The system is set up for us, and it often gives us power without us even having to ask for it. We can be White without ever thinking about being White. To be fair, the church is not alone in mindlessly offering this message. Hollywood loves to tell White savior stories rather than stories of strength within cultures unattached to the people group in power. The news media is no better.

For the White hands who hold the reins of historical and institutional power, it boils down to this: We want to say that everything that happens in church is about Jesus, but it's simply not. We have to acknowledge cultural, historical, and social structures that shape our thinking and contribute to the breakdown of Christian unity.

We say we want to be a "church of many nations," and we cheer for videos like the one mentioned; but sometimes our arrogance, ignorance, and unwillingness to listen communicates that we really view "the nations" as our subjects, not as our partners, existing to make us look good and serve our own end.

- Put the Black guy on stage to read the Martin Luther King, Jr. Day prayer = *We will give lip service to civil rights rather than pursue justice and equality.*
- Take pictures of minorities in our institution to display prominently in our publications = *We support the appearance of diversity, but may or may not support you, especially if you say things contradictory to our established norms.*
- Sing White hipster music in Spanish = *We want to appear inclusive of all languages and cultures yet also communicate, "You, too, can be just like me, even in your language!"*
- Host an international event with ethnic food and clothing = *We appear to accept different backgrounds but simply skim the surface and maintain a safe distance from the complexities and harder realities of real relationship.*
- Send brochures with hungry-looking poor children = *We want to communicate we care about the poor but also intend to exploit guilty feelings.*

I know this all sounds harsh and a bit cynical. I've been right there with you, defending myself, confident of my pure intentions. However, regardless of our intentions, the impact of our actions can be isolating and downright hurtful to people of color. White people, especially those in Christian leadership, need to start acknowledging this and listening to others with utmost seriousness. This conversation cannot flow in one direction only. If we do not listen to the voices that courageously share their experience with us, we are breaking the very body we so sincerely wish to build.

“Cultural competency” is a popular term these days, and, while I appreciate the sentiment of the phrase, I wonder whether it’s helpful. When it comes to race relations, I think we should expect *some* incompetence. For instance, I once mistook an Iranian student for an Egyptian and suspected immediately that I’d offended him. I hadn’t meant to—I’d confused him with another student—but I couldn’t take my words back either. I didn’t know enough about Middle Eastern culture to know the degree to which my mistake was offensive. After stumbling around a little, attempting to retract my words, I gave up trying to defend my incompetence. “I’m sorry,” I admitted. “I didn’t know. Please forgive my mistake.”

A colleague recently introduced me to the term *cultural humility*, and I instantly connected to it. I think it’s far more helpful than *competency*. Even with all my hard-earned competencies—being married cross-culturally, earning a degree in multicultural education, speaking several languages, travelling on five continents, and spending my days with immigrants from around the world—I often feel culturally incompetent. I only speak two languages fluently, not six, like some of my students. I grew up in a monocultural cornfield and have had to work hard to learn about the rest of the world. I have always lived in my country of birth and don’t have the depth of experience or insight about cultural adjustment that the world’s resilient immigrants know.

Culturally, I am far from competent. But cultural *humility*? That makes sense to me.

Instead of "Get over it!", cultural humility responds, "I don't understand. Can you help me understand more deeply?"

Instead of replying with some variation of "quit whining" to someone who feels wronged, cultural humility responds, "I'm so sorry this hurts you. How can I walk alongside you in this? What do I need to learn?"

Instead of reading and listening to only the White megachurch types, cultural humility also seeks wisdom from Christian leaders from a wide variety of cultural, theological, and ethnic backgrounds.

Instead of saying, "Why do you keep causing problems?", cultural humility responds, "I'm sorry I keep hurting you. It seems like I'm missing something big. How would you recommend I start to better understand your experience?"

Instead of keeping quiet because of ignorance, cultural humility clumsily admits, "I'm a little embarrassed that I don't know much about your background. I don't even know how to ask you questions about it, but I would love to learn more."

While all of this might sound a lot like an us-vs-them scenario, it does not have to be. While I have never lived in a different skin, I fiercely love those who do. I share my perspective here as a bridge between worlds for I long to see those on both sides listen to and love each other so much better than we currently do.

When White people don't recognize how our position of cultural dominance influences and even benefits us—that is, *when we don't know that we're being White*—we can act like bulls in a china shop, throwing our weight around in damaging ways without even realizing what we're doing. For us, this understanding begins with learning and practicing a discipline of cultural humility and seeking to understand another's experience without judgment. May more of us boldly begin to walk on this long and winding path.

Ponder.

1. Did the phrase "cultural humility" strike a particular chord for you? What type of emotion did it stir? What do you think cultural humility looks like in practice? How might you learn more about being culturally humble?
2. What is your first reaction to discussions of racial inequality? Why do you think you react this way?
3. How familiar are you with the lived experience of people of color? What do you feel that you already know? What might you need to learn more about?
4. What does 'cultural dominance' look like to you? What might it look like to others?

2

The Painful Realities of White Privilege

We were sitting at the frozen yogurt shop when my husband interrupted my yogurt induced heaven with a passionate "Did you see that?!"

"What?" I looked around but didn't see anything unusual. I'd been a little spaced out in a blissful yogurt coma and was, as usual, less than aware of my surroundings.

"That Asian lady in the yogurt store! She and her daughter were just standing there, waiting in line for the restroom, and this White guy came in and walked *right* in front of her."

He paused, shaking his head in angry disbelief, "And she just *let* him go. She put her head down and let him push his way past her."

He paused, processing the interaction, "That's just *so privileged,* and he probably doesn't even recognize it! The problem with us is that we get all submissive and let people walk all over us."

Confession Time: In my head, I started listing all the reasons why what he just said happened couldn't have actually happened. Maybe he saw things wrong. Maybe the guy had to puke. Maybe he left his cell phone in the bathroom. Surely what my husband saw wasn't what *actually* happened.

But then I remembered what I've learned about race and privilege: dismissing perceptions is one of the most unhelpful responses in race conversations.

I should already know this, right?

Right.

(Except that I don't always remember it at the right times.)

Privilege runs deep, and, as I continue to ponder the ideas of humility, I keep running smack into its gritty realities. They're not pretty, but ignoring them won't make them go away either. Here are a few truths I've learned along the way:

Privilege is hard to see if you have it, but easy to see if you don't.

I often don't see the privilege my husband or my friends of color see, but not because it doesn't exist. I don't see it because I don't *have* to see it. I live in a world where people who look like me carry the heaviest influence, so the world-at-large adjusts to me, not the other way around. I can walk into a restaurant without heads turning in curiosity. I can shop in a thrift store and people may well assume I'm cool, not poor. People on the street will never assume I look 'suspicious'. I've never encountered a situation where people define my personal qualifications by my physical appearance. People rarely make comments—ignorant or informed—about my race or ethnic background.

It reminds me of the emperor who wasn't wearing any clothes—everyone but the stubborn king sees the truth. I can almost hear that classic fairytale character, walking naked down the street, thinking to himself as the little boy called his bluff, "That crazy boy! Who does he think he is? He doesn't know anything. I'm the Emperor, after all. What I say goes!"

It's not so different from the knee-jerk reaction that many White people have when confronted with the concept of White privilege:

> *"Who do they think they are?"* We think about the people of color who suggest perspectives that overturn our understanding of the world.
>
> *"What do they know?"* We tell ourselves as a means of dismissing the realities they share. When those of us in power write history without considering other sides of the story, we can find it impossible to understand why some might question our interpretation of it.

If I'm brutally honest with myself, I've done the same thing as the privileged White guy at the yogurt shop and never even noticed. Privilege just doesn't feel the same to those who benefit from it like it does to those who get run over by it.

Privilege feels great and horrible at the same time.

I'll be the first to say that being the one with the power feels great. Power is fun, but an equal reality of power is that it corrupts and blinds. The power that privilege carries does this as well. That's why the headlines erupt over public justifications of privilege[3] and racial debates rage between opposing factions. It's an intensely divisive topic, creating fierce discussion regarding its actual existence.

When I travel, I am nearly always treated better than my non-White family. I get higher quality service, more attention and courtesy. I get less attention at airport security lines and from policemen. Even if I personally benefit from this treatment, the fact that my family faces its fallout sours any positives it holds for me. If people knew how much more humble, sacrificial, and generous my non-white family is than me, they would be the ones given elevated status, not me.

Privilege creates guilt, which creates shame, which creates denial.

Author and researcher, Brené Brown, has shed an immense amount of light on how shame impacts our ability to be vulnerable; and it's easily applicable when considering privilege. She writes:

> Owning our story can be hard but not nearly as difficult as spending our lives running from it. Embracing our vulnerabilities is risky but not nearly as dangerous as

> giving up on love and belonging and joy—the experiences that make us the most vulnerable. Only when we are brave enough to explore the darkness will we discover the infinite power of our light.[4]

When I don't initially understand a situation like the yogurt shop, I can take weeks to admit it. My guilt kicks in...how many years have I been married interracially? How many conversations have I had and books have I read about exploring the darkness of my own history and privilege?

Will I ever learn?

The shame lingers so subtly that I don't even notice it until my denial eventually slips out, and I'm forced to face my privilege once again.

Privilege isn't about individuals, it's about systems.

Conversations about privilege often don't acknowledge that privilege is not necessarily applicable to individuals. The recent attention to the idea of microagressions—subtle and subconscious acts of prejudice—highlights how systems impact individuals. When microaggressions play out on an individual level, they trigger reactions because of the history such interactions carry with them.

In other words, when the White guy marches past the Asian lady in the restroom line, the history of White-dominant/Asian-submissive interaction plops down right into the center of things.

The same thing can happen when the media paints a picture that all Africans live in destitute poverty or when someone ignorantly assumes that people who aren't White don't speak English well. Although we'd like to believe otherwise, the world is not only made up of individuals, it's also composed of groups who represent ideas and create realities beyond individuals' control.

Privilege isn't only about race.

As I grow in my understanding of privilege, I see how it extends far beyond the context of race. Privilege comes in many packages and shapes how we view and interact with the world.

"I am unlearning the ways I perceive my own areas of privilege as 'normal'," writes Austin Channing. "I can smell when patriarchy is leaking all over a man as he interacts with me. But there are plenty of other ways that I engage in oppression, ignorance, avoidance, and all kinds of crazy."[5]

I think of all the times I fail to consider other realities—realities of disability, education level, class, language ability, religious views, or sexual orientation, and subconsciously operate as though mine is the norm. There are multiple ways in which I exclude the "other" and see myself as the one who belongs.

Examining how I engage with people of different backgrounds is critical to the development of the model of humility in Philippians 2:

> *"If you've gotten anything at all out of following Christ, if his love has made any difference in your life, if being in a community of the Spirit means anything to you, if you have a heart, if you care—then do me a favor: Agree with each other, love each other, be deep-spirited friends. Don't push your way to the front; don't sweet-talk your way to the top. Put yourself aside, and help others get ahead. Don't be obsessed with getting your own advantage. Forget yourselves long enough to lend a helping hand.*
>
> *Think of yourselves the way Christ Jesus thought of himself. He had equal status with God but didn't think so much of himself that he had to cling to the advantages of that status no matter what. Not at all. When the time came, he set aside the privileges of deity and took on the status of a slave, became human! Having become human, he stayed human. It was an incredibly humbling process. He didn't claim special privileges. Instead, he lived a selfless, obedient life and then died a selfless, obedient death—and the worst kind of death at that—a crucifixion."* (The Message)

Christ's example stands in stark contrast to the pundits and pontificators who insist nothing-is-wrong-with-me in response to the racial struggles of our world. It sheds new light on the pushy White guy's behavior in the yogurt line. It opens the heart's door of this stubbornly-skeptical woman just a teeny-bit wider.

Our world is sorely in need of people who follow Christ before they follow political figures and tribe leaders. When we fight against the privilege discussion because it's too painful to face the reality of the broken history and systems of our world, we end up perpetuating the exact same legacy.

Instead, may our humility grow deep enough that we have the courage to walk through the painful realities privilege carries. May we, like Christ, live selflessly and obediently rather than clinging to privilege and status. If we truly want to see change in the world, we must first begin with ourselves.

Ponder.

1. Which reality discussed in this chapter makes the most sense to you? Which is the most difficult to understand?
2. Reflect on the Philippians 2 passage, noticing which phrases stick out to you. Ask God to show you how you might better live out these words with those around you.

3

Myths and Emotions that Keep White People from Talking about Race

While much has improved since the days of segregation laws and public lynchings, racism has by no means gone away. As racial conflicts unfold with increasingly regularity, I take them in with a sense of shock and sorrow. Conservative pundits' accusations of 'race baiting' and 'playing the race card' capture headlines, but a less publicized, more complex story I hear from White people around me is a sad confusion over the continued existence of racism. I've found myself overwhelmed by this confusion to the point of checking out completely. While self-care is sometimes necessary for those deeply involved in difficult conversations, I'm keenly aware that it's far too easy for me to avoid facing race because I don't have to care; my skin gives me that option.

In her article, *White People Facing Race: Uncovering Myths that Keep Racism in Place,* Peggy McIntosh examines myths that keep White people from understanding the experience of other races.[6] Understanding these assumptions and the emotions associated with them has helped me shift my mindset when I find myself wanting to disengage from the on-going racial conflict in our country.

Guilt and the Myth of Meritocracy

"I am tired of this guilty conscience mentality that people are trying to push onto White people," wrote a commenter on one of my blog posts about race. He is certainly not alone. I have heard many White people understandably express frustration with feeling forced to take responsibility for past actions for which they are not responsible. Since we have no control over our ancestors' choices, why should we be blamed for them?

Beverly Tatum, author of *Why do all the Black kids sit together in the cafeteria,* suggests that White society's primary understanding of itself as composed of individuals in a meritocracy prevents many from seeing systemic racism.[7] In other words, we think we got where we are all by ourselves and that we deserve it. This individualistic mindset contrasts significantly with the perspective of many people of color who come from communal cultures that view individual success as rooted in the experience of a surrounding community.

Individualism influences the White evangelical church in America in ways it has not acknowledged. For example, this arm of the church disproportionately focuses on individual sins relating to sex like homosexuality, abortion, and pre-marital sex while often turning a blind eye to corporate sins like greed, lack of care for the poor, causes of poverty, and preferential laws for the rich.

When we view ourselves as individuals and not part of a whole, it's easy for accusations of racism to induce guilt. It's true—*we didn't* do it individually. However, when we consider the perspective of communally-oriented cultures, we learn more about how we, as individuals, are situated in a system established to benefit us at the expense of others. We live, happily oblivious, in a system in which we quite comfortably tell *our* stories from *our* perspectives far more frequently than any others. Acknowledging the imbalance of this system opens our minds to consider how we will continue to perpetrate this very system unless we make intentional actions to change it.

In a majority world, individuals are viewed as the sole component of society. There are no *groups*, only *people*. As a result, people get what they want and deserve based on their individual choices. The American mantra of 'pulling yourself up by your bootstraps' reinforces this sentiment: all you have to do is try and you'll succeed because nothing stands in your way. There is little acknowledgment of the impact that systems have on individuals.

Ponder.

1. How might the Thanksgiving story be told from a Native American perspective? Could it be perceived differently than a peaceful dinner between the Indian and the White

Man? Explore a different narrative by searching the internet to look for Native American perspectives on the traditional Thanksgiving story.

2. Which voices frame the theological story we tell? How would that story be told differently from those of a non-dominant power?

3. Where are our theories rooted? If the research on which we base our understanding of 'sound theory' comes only from a White western perspective, what realities might we be missing?

4. If I feel afraid or guilty in race conversations, how have I dealt with these emotions? Do I allow them to immobilize me or do I lean into them as opportunities for growth?

Arrogance and the Myth of White Moral Elevation

If I am really honest with myself, I kind of like the position of racial privilege that comes with my skin color/tone. Plain and simple, there are significant advantages to being White. This doesn't mean that I consciously believe I deserve it or that I'm better because of my race, but it is a reality in my thinking that is important to recognize. One of my blog readers summed up this sense well:

> *I think part of my fallen culture as a White privileged male person is to use my power to control and fix things and people. It's quite likely that that's a bigger part of my draw to working with people from other cultures than I'd care*

> *to admit. But I need to confess this, continually, and claim my call as faithfulness, not fixing. I fail. Maybe we need a WPA (White privilege anonymous: "Hi, I'm Jim, and I'm privileged"). Actually doing my own "White work" and engaging privilege directly is much harder for me than "serving" folks from other cultures.*

Sometimes, we just need to listen humbly, surrender our need to be the center of attention, and keep our mouths shut. Being honest about our own subtle arrogance and preference for power is a great starting point toward humility for us all. Beverly Tatum discusses the necessity of courage to break the silence in the race conversation, "Silence feels safer, but in the long run, I know it is not." She recognizes that nothing will happen if she acquiesces to her fear of confronting the reality she sees and that silence is ultimately not a beneficial response for herself personally or society at large.[8]

When White people avoid facing their own arrogance and the privileges that historical systems have afforded them, we only continue the story. If we want to be part of the healing of the racially scarred history of our country, the conversation must first begin within our own hearts.

Ponder.

1. Can you think of a time you felt subconsciously superior to someone else? Be honest about your feelings and the situation, then consider why you felt this way.

2. What kind of things do you talk about that you don't really know? Resolve to practice quietness and listening in these areas.

3. How do I respond when someone presents a perspective I don't understand? If I am defensive, dismissive, or angry, why? What prevents me from hearing their story? How might I learn to respond with more compassion?

4. In conversations about race, do I listen or do I preach? Do I assume that I am right? Do I follow Stephen Covey's model and listen, first to understand, then to be understood, or do I leave the conversation before I even consider the other participant's perspective?

National Pride and the Myth of Manifest Destiny

Because racism is embedded so deeply in the foundations of our country, it remains difficult for those who have traditionally held the power to recognize it. The history lesson of *Manifest Destiny* teaches that God gave this land to America, and that we are, as a result, his chosen people. Seeing the US as "a nation chosen by God" keeps us from acknowledging the long-term impact of the blatantly evil and racist history of Native American genocide, African slavery, Japanese internment, and segregation laws.

While we might not see blatantly racist signs like "Keep California ", "Whites only", or "Get 'em outta here" as frequently as in decades past, their sentiment remains pervasive in the hearts of many. Current issues like school segregation, urban gentrification, and White-boy-club politics demonstrate ways in which racial dynamics continue to divide our country.

Frontline recently did an investigation of school segregation that revealed the continued divide in America's public schools among races and economic classes. The study showed a steady decline in progress by Black students in the south since the 1990s. It also highlighted the court's propensity to steer clear of such cases as well as White students' lack of interaction with students of color in school settings.[9]

As cities have grown in popularity with young urban professionals, neighborhoods that were once considered *rough* are now considered *hip*. This process of urban development, or *gentrification*, can create complicated relationships between young hipsters and long-time residents. While newcomers to a neighborhood might feel that calls for development improve the neighborhood, long-time residents can also feel dismissed and undervalued when the neighborhood shifts in tone, regulation, and tax base.[10]

Finally, the challenge of all-White leadership persists. Even if churches or other Christian organizations claim to value diverse perspectives, the leadership still reflects mostly White faces and perspectives. Some people of color within White-dominant institutions have courageously shared their stories. In his book, *Reconciliation Blues: A Black Evangelical's Inside View of White Christianity,* Edward Gilbreath shares the perspective of a young friend:

> *The White Christians I encounter often display a shocking provincialism—a real naiveté about the world around them. Frankly, it's as if they are stunned to find out that their cultural, political, and religious frame of reference is not the only one.*[11]

Gilbreath reflects further on his own experience with conservative White Christians, "Sometimes I get the feeling that some White evangelicals won't consider an African American believer a real Christian unless he or she subscribes to their conservative political views."[12]

Each of these examples demonstrates ways in which damage occurs when White people fail to recognize how our rootedness in concepts of manifest destiny and privilege impact societal and relational dynamics. They also highlight the complexities of healing a nation established on racist ideologies.

Ponder.

1. Do you feel naïve? What steps could you take to become more informed about racial and cultural dynamics in society?
2. What do you know about your own cultural history? Where do you come from? What shapes your subconscious values and rules?
3. What do you know about the history of other races and cultures? How do you know this history? Was it told through the eyes of the culture itself or the dominant

culture? Could there be another perspective than the one you've been taught?

Ignorance and the Myth of White Racelessness

To put it bluntly, a lot of White people don't talk about race because they don't know how or because they assume that just because they've had a few conversations or watched some news clips, they know enough to have an opinion about the topic.

When discussing race, many White people struggle to identify cultural characteristics they share with other Whites. Growing up as a member of the majority can foster an "I don't have a culture—I'm just normal" perspective that assumes race only applies to other people.

Additionally, White people's participation in racial oppression isn't seen as an act of racism, but simply as normal. We see it time and again through the merchandising of products like nude pantyhose and flesh colored crayons that are pale-peach. We see it in advertisements that include only White faces and public response to shootings-by-White-people versus shootings-by-Brown-people. When Brown people do something bad, it's immediately attributed to their race. When White people do something bad, their race is not mentioned.

For White people to grasp racial dynamics, it's crucial that they first understand the role that our own race plays in society and history. Failing to face these realities creates a short-sighted and ignorant perspective that will only serve to repeat history, not redeem it.

In college, I was on a committee to plan the Martin Luther King Jr. Day celebration on campus. Our (mostly White) committee came up with the slogan, "Racism: Been there, done that." When we suggested our theme to the invited African American speaker, she pushed back. "Oh no, you haven't!" she countered, and she was quite right. We thought that our willingness to say the word *race* meant that we actually knew something about it. How wrong we were.

Statements like, "The problem is that minorities keep themselves segregated" or "I'm colorblind. I don't see race" illustrate an ignorance that many White people continue to believe. We may believe it because:

1. we operate on media driven sound bites or stereotypes;
2. we don't have actual friends of other races;
3. we rely on our own experience and not fact;
4. we apply limited interactions with people of color to *all* people of color;
5. we don't believe experiences except those that reflect our own.

When someone's assumption about the motives behind the actions of other races are misguided, their views will be slow to change until they dig deeper than the reasons above.

Gary Howard wrote an insightful book for teachers called, *We can't teach what we don't know: White teachers, multiracial schools.* In a similar vein, we can't talk about what we don't know.[13] Until we've spent significant time understanding both our own attitudes and the perspectives of others in the racial conversation, we remain only observers of the conversation, not true participants in it. We can't simply will ignorance away. If we want to increase our understanding, we have to do something about it.

Groupthink and the Myth of Monoculture

Viewing values through a single lens leads many to operate on the assumption that there is one "American" culture that everyone experiences in similar ways. This is still the myth I catch myself practicing most frequently when I slip up and make comments like, "Christians think..." or "Americans say..." when what I really mean is "White evangelical Christians in the Midwest think..." or "White middle-class Americans say..." Making statements like this that lump everyone into one group creates an unspoken expectation that people of color adapt to the "White way" and cave to the majority assumptions that everyone is just like them.

Christena Cleveland explores this compulsion to divide and categorize in her book, *Disunity in Christ: Uncovering the hidden forces that keep us apart.* She asserts that dividing and categorizing fosters an us vs. them mentality which in turn promotes an exaggeration of difference so that each group feels better about their unique characteristics. The problem with this process is that it creates a group dynamic that establishes its own standards as normal.[14] Racially, we see this most frequently when White churches or organizations operate using a very 'White style' that invariably leaves people of color feeling excluded. This happens most frequently with musical styles but also extends to other areas like preaching styles and political values as well.

In my household, I am occasionally teased for listening to 'White music'. Because of my upbringing, musical styles along the lines of Rich Mullins and Amy Grant still tug at my heartstrings. For a while, it was tempting to reject my musical preference because of my family's distaste for it, but over time, I realized that it was simply part of my spiritual DNA. I came to accept it for what it was—meaningful to me, but not so much to others. As a result of our stylistic differences, I also learned to appreciate other kinds of music that my family enjoyed as well. My experience in my own family is a microcosm of what could happen in the church—shared stories, different styles, and patient appreciation for one another's histories.

To consider others better than ourselves à la Philippians 2 requires that we don't unintentionally demand others follow cultural norms that we don't even realize we have. It also requires that we consider the differences that present themselves through how we view diverse perspectives on theology, worship style, or individual spiritual expression.

Ponder.

1. While the White perspective shouldn't be eliminated, an accurate overarching story should include a wide array of

perspectives that extend beyond the dominant group. How could you (or your church or organization) incorporate broader stories than you currently do?

2. How do you identify to the us-vs-them mentality? Are there rules you've been operating by that may be interpreted differently by others?

Self-righteousness and the Myth of White Moral Elevation

Years ago, I chaperoned a diverse group of high school students on a field trip to the nation's Capital Building. I grew quickly ashamed when I saw painting after painting of White men. Where were the role models that reflected the backgrounds of my students of color? What possibilities could they imagine for themselves if the only people credited with America's greatness looked nothing like them? Why had the history of their backgrounds been ignored?

The myth of White moral elevation tells a story with White people at the center of all good decisions and critical points in history. It makes White people the perpetual winner in every conflict and paints non-White parties as criminals, bystanders, or victims.

Telling stories with White saviors at the helm creates a societal bias that fosters a subconscious superiority complex. Media, education, and society implicitly communicate this bias by acting as though it is exceptional for people of color to be in the limelight. This attitude comes through in statements like, "He's so articulate" or "She doesn't act Black" that express surprise when a person of color doesn't fit a societal stereotype. We see it time and again in our church leadership structures, elected political officers, and community leaders. Even in the most diverse regions of the country, the majority of people who pull the power-making strings are White.

To truly grapple with how this self-righteous perspective impacts society and ourselves, we need to regularly ask why this reality still characterizes one of the most diverse countries in the world. While this is only the beginning of the conversation, it's a great place to begin. Understanding race is not a one-time-thing. It is a never-ending process of listening and learning in order to become a safe place to hold the stories of those around us with gentler hands.

Ponder.

1. Consider which myth you have believed most strongly. If this is truly a myth, how would views that you currently hold change?
2. Which myth is hardest for you to grasp? What kind of experience would make this myth easier to understand?
3. Which emotion hits you the hardest? How does this emotion affect your reaction to how you think about race?

4

Why White People Need to Talk about Race

Hi. My name is Jody, and I'm White.

Over the years, this single admission has often felt like an Alcoholics Anonymous confession, a fact about which I can do nothing and for which I am slightly ashamed. I have stood at bus stops in Black neighborhoods on the south side of Chicago, desperately wishing for dreads and dark skin so I wouldn't stand out so starkly. I have maneuvered the streets of the developing world being greeted with solicitations like "I lofe you, babeee" and "Taxi, madam" because of the color of my skin. I have received unwanted but superior treatment because my skin defines me as a wealthy foreigner.

My Whiteness is something I did not ask for, cannot change, and don't completely understand. While I haven't always been aware of the full implications of this trait in a racialized society, living between worlds has pushed me to grapple with my race as a significant shaper of my identity. As I began this process, there was a time when I was ashamed of the privilege I carried, angered and saddened by the history of racial supremacy and discrimination. I hear this shame frequently from other White people, frustrated with feeling blamed, dismissed, or responsible for actions-not-their-own. In response to a post on my blog about racial issues, one reader articulated a sentiment I often hear from White people:

> *I feel frustrated that I somehow inherited qualities based on what my race did or didn't do, and that I have "responsibilities" to be a certain way to other races therefore. I feel people want me to feel guilty for who I am based solely on my race.*
>
> *I'm tired of being the bad guy, the boring guy, the rich guy, whatever. I'm tired of being told I have no right to feel that way because others have it worse. I'm tired of being singled out, having to be taught how to be "culturally sensitive" as if I'm the only one who isn't—which incidentally reinforces privilege. I'm tired of being told I can't have a voice, an opinion.*

Another commenter shared a similar opinion:

> *Assuming someone's Whiteness or Blackness marks their cultural makeup and place in society does not further the discussion nor lead to constructive debate. The issue in claiming that White people should burden the responsibility is that we again draw swords for the wrong reasons.*
>
> *We entrench ourselves in our values and take sides to eliminate the burden of guilt and point to a symbol, which has no clear identity, as the root of the problem. Respect, faith, and personal responsibility should be a driving force*

> *in how people conduct themselves with any and every person regardless of race.*

Comments like these highlight the discomfort, insecurity, ignorance, and fear that many White people feel when talking about race. These reactions indicate why it is crucial that we need to speak about it more than we do.

We are uncomfortable when we talk about race.

It's rare that I hear a White person use the word "Black" in public settings to describe someone's race without stuttering in the process. Most White people stumble nervously over themselves when using racial terms, "She's a-um-a, well, she's af-, bl-um, she's BlackImeanAfric-um, I mean, African American?"

Yeah. Let's just be honest—I know I've done it; and I know that chances are most White folks reading this have done it too. We're uncomfortable using racial terms because we don't think in racial terms on a regular basis.

People of color think and talk about race *all the time*—they have to in order to negotiate living in a world where the dominant power structure does not validate cultural norms outside of its own. When race is a daily factor in human relations, people develop the language and ability to process it. However, because White people remain so silent and ignorant on the issue, we often don't have a clue as to how to talk about race with someone from a different background.

Ponder.

1. How was race discussed in your family of origin? How does this impact how you speak about race?
2. How do you speak about race with other White people?
3. Are you comfortable talking about race in the presence of those from other races? Why do you think you feel this way?
4. If race comes up in a conversation, either positively or negatively, do you speak or remain silent? Why do you respond the way you do?

We don't know who we are.

I (along with plenty of other scholars) would argue that one of the reasons we defend ourselves so vigorously is because we don't fully understand how our perspectives are shaped by racial dynamics. Beverly Daniel Tatum suggests that the silence on race in White communities stems from the fact that White people see race as a defining trait for other people, not themselves.[15] As one White student commented, "I'm not White, I'm just normal."

Tatum then goes on to explain the stages of White identity development, something I'd never even heard of until my college years. My first encounter with my Whiteness was when I participated in an urban studies program on the south side of Chicago. We privileged and White college students lived in a rehab center with recovering drug addicts, all of whom were

African Americans from urban Chicago neighborhoods. Completely unaware of the cultural rules by which I operated, I dove into seeking relationship with the residents, eager to learn more about their lives. I asked all sorts of questions and listened eagerly as they shared their stories with me, a naïve rural White girl.

I thought I was maneuvering just fine until one day, a woman approached me and said, "I need to apologize to you. I've been avoiding you the whole time you've been here."

I froze inside, wondering what I'd done wrong. People where I came from were rarely so blunt. I thought I'd been so nice—listening, smiling, asking questions. I wasn't sure how to respond to her bluntness; so I just continued to listen. "You asked so many questions, I felt like you were some journalist pelting me with questions," she explained. "It didn't feel like you really wanted to know me, just like you wanted to use me for my stories."

I thought I might cry, both from her misinterpretation of my intentions and my lack of understanding about how my actions had been perceived.

"So, I'm sorry," she said. "I'm sorry I didn't give you a chance and just shut down on you instead. It wasn't very nice of me."

I stumbled through some sort of response, but mostly I was speechless because I didn't know what to say. It was the first time I'd come face-to-face with a person whose cultural rules dictated different values than mine, and I hadn't even known I'd been operating by cultural rules. In my mind, I was just being *normal*.

What I was learning for the first time is that *normal* isn't the same for everyone. Gerald Pine and Asa Hilliard explain some of the underlying dynamics shaping our differing communication styles:

> *Discussions and debates about racism create anxiety and conflict, which are handled differently by different cultural groups. For example, Whites tend to fear open discussion of racial problems because they believe that such discussion will stir up hard feelings and old hatreds. Whites tend to believe that heated arguments about racism lead to divisiveness, loss of control, bitter conflict, and even violence. Blacks, on the other hand, believe that discussion and debate about racism help to push racial problems to the surface – and perhaps, force society to deal with them.*[16]

When I hear Whites portray themselves as 'colorblind', I think of myself in those days, unaware and shielded from the harsh realities surrounding race and privilege as well as the different values by which I operated.

I think of the friend who said to me, "If you don't see my color, you don't see me." I think of all the people who feel silenced in the race conversation because they feel blamed, misportrayed, or pigeon-holed. I think of the intense individualism by which White mainstream America unknowingly operates that conflicts with the communal value systems of other races and cultures. And then I think it would do us all a whole-lot-of-good to talk about these things far more than we do.

Ponder.

1. Have you had negative experiences in talking about race? What happened? How did you respond? How could you have responded differently?
2. Do some internet research on White Identity Development. What stage are you currently in? Brainstorm some ways you might continue to develop a deeper understanding of White identity.

We need healing, too.

Oppression does not only hurt the oppressed, it leaves deep scars on the oppressor as well. Silence breeds shame, and the silence about our history as racial oppressors has allowed our shame to work its way so deeply into our culture that we don't even see how it eats away at us. Some of us even find it funny when it shows up in our private-little-racial-jokes or from shock jock personalities like Rush Limbaugh. If Donald Trump has given the American public one gift, it is ripping the façade off our belief that racism is a thing of the past.

In contrast, however, many white people have watched the events in Ferguson and Charleston with broken hearts and tear-stained cheeks. We've longed for change to occur but feel overwhelmed, distant, and helpless. Quite frankly, sometimes it all feels like one big messy subject, a conflict too painful to solve, more divisive than uniting.

But Parker Palmer's words linger in my heart, "We think the world apart, what would it be like to think the world together?"[17] This is where healing for everyone begins in this complex conversation; to think the world together, there need to be *two* participants in the conversation. If we truly want to see change (which I believe many of us do), it can't just be the people of color who are invested in this issue. When White people "participate" in the conversation by smugly crossing our arms, silently observing from a distance, assuming we know better, or arrogantly refusing to consider other perspectives, we only perpetuate the system we've inherited.

Ponder.

1. Is silence about race part of your story? If so, what feelings arise when you start to talk or think about it?
2. How are you invested in racial issues? How might you become more involved?
3. Who are the people you know well? Are your social circles made up of mostly people just like you? If so, have you ever really listened to someone's story that does not reflect your own?

We're afraid of conflict.

Perhaps the most potent reason White people don't talk about race is fear of conflict. This can be fear of both internal and external conflict. A commenter on my blog writes about this fear:

> *Yes, racism is real in the United States, as is privilege, but I think there has to be a way to deal with that problem without constantly having to take the posture of being apologetic so that everyone knows you're not like those "other" culturally insensitive people.*

This comment summarizes well the fear that many White people have of being wrong, looking ignorant, or saying the wrong thing in conversations about race.

Dr. Sarah Visser, a scholar of diversity and White privilege, points out that this fear of conflict need not be only with others. "I think that often when we experience fear-triggers, we assume that it's coming from someone or something," she wrote in an email exchange we had on the topic, "when actually it springs from deep inside us and is evidence of our need to do some personal work."[18]

I learn this lesson time and again, not realizing the impact of a racialized society on my own thinking. Years ago, I was teaching at a very diverse high school. One of my best students was a tall African American male who faithfully submitted meticulous work, treated everyone with respect, and was well-known for his kind and gentle manner. One morning, I was walking into school and saw a large Black male dressed in saggy pants, an oversized jersey, and a cock-eyed hat. Instantly, I tensed because of the 'gangsta' image I perceived from afar. As I walked closer, I recognized him as my beloved, straight-A student.

Coming face to face with my subconscious absorption of society's stereotypes of Black male youth, I was both shocked and embarrassed by my reaction. Despite what I thought I believed, I was not at all immune to subscribing to stereotypes. In order to deal with this stereotype I held, it was necessary for me to intentionally acknowledge it, even if only to myself, rather than remain silent to save face.

Ponder.

1. How does your family of origin handle conflict? Do you handle conflict in a similar or different way than what you saw as a child?
2. How do others you know handle conflict? If they handle it differently than you do, speculate on why that might be the case.
3. If you've experienced conflict in conversations about race, try to identify what causes the fear. Are you defensive, afraid of being wrong, losing control, etc.?

5

Tips to Help White People Talk about Race

It's no secret that race is a polarizing topic to discuss. Given White people's history of being the oppressor, it's an even harder issue for us to talk about. As a group, we tend to either stay quiet on the issue out of ignorance/fear, defend ourselves, or flip out and do horribly offensive things that make us look like racist fools. Such black-and-white responses do little to heal race relations; we need some new ways to respond to this topic.

One of the most common reasons I hear White people say they don't talk about race is fear of saying the wrong thing. I know many people who don't want to be offensive, but who also simply have no idea how to enter a conversation about race because they've never had one. They may care deeply about people, but, without experience or understanding of race in their own lives, they bumble through such conversations, hoping for the best but not really knowing if they're helping or hurting.

These tips on talking about race will offer a starting point for people who want to be part of the solution instead of the problem.

Listen.

In many race conversations, the dominant group is eager to share their opinions, views, or perceptions of how they see things. They begin conversations by stating their questions, observations, or disagreements with a presumption of 'rightness' and give an unspoken impression that there's no possible way to have a different perception other than their own.

By participating in conversations first by listening, requesting clarification, and listening again, we communicate openness and allow ourselves to actually hear the reality of another's experience instead of shutting down the conversation by becoming defensive, dismissive, or dominant. When people with power take the initiative to speak last (or sometimes, not at all), they communicate a humility that opens doors rather than closes them.

After the Charleston shooting of nine people at a historic African American church in 2013, writer Osheta Moore suggests that a response of "I'm listening" should be a starting point for public response to tragic headlines:

> *We're called to be reconcilers. Like Jesus reconciled us to the Father—it's a painful process. A denying process. A humiliating process. But a Kingdom process, nonetheless. "I'm listening" says, "yes, I have an opinion and yes I have strong feelings, and yes this makes me feel more than a little helpless, but I'm going to press into this specific pain and listen."*[19]

Ponder.

1. What is your natural response in conversations? Are you a listener or a talker? Ask others close to you if they perceive you in the same way as you perceive yourself.
2. Have you ever sat and listened to a conversation about racial issues without commenting? If yes, what did you learn? If no, brainstorm ways you might find an opportunity to do this.

Learn.

Factually speaking, White people don't have any idea what it means to live as a racial minority in a racialized society. We can't. The simple fact that we're White means we don't experience racial prejudice firsthand on a regular basis. However, even if we don't understand from personal experience, we can attempt to learn more about what it means to see through someone else's eyes. With the sheer availability and accessibility of media today, we have no excuse to not read, watch movies, or seek out viewpoints outside of our own experience. If we want to be a valuable participant in the conversation, we need to speak from a place of awareness, not ignorance.

Seeking out other White people who are further along the path of racial understanding to process with in this phase is important to note at this stage. Quite frankly, too many eager-but-stupid-White-folk can be completely exhausting for the people of color who consistently have to dialogue about issues of race or who may be working through challenging points in their own process of racial identity development. William A. Smith coined this experience *racial battle fatigue,* a term which nails the overwhelming emotion many people of color face when they have to continually challenge others to acknowledge the realities of racism.[20] Most White people who understand privilege, however, have been racially ignorant themselves at some point and have an ability to understand and empathize with those just beginning the path.

Ponder.

1. Which ways listed below would be most helpful/realistic for you to learn more about race?

    - Watching movies/documentaries
    - Reading books/articles
    - Traveling
    - Attending an event targeted toward a different ethnicity (e.g. church, music concert, lecture, festival, etc.)
    - Engaging friends of other races
    - Volunteering

2. Do some research on your choices and then write three specific goals you have for implementing the above into your life. For example, what specific movies will you

watch, which friends will you engage, where will you volunteer, etc. (See *Appendix A, B,* and *C for more ideas).*

Accept.

I've had more success accepting realities present in racial conversations when I've acknowledged my ignorance rather than attempting to defeat or discount them. When I know my knowledge is inadequate, I'll start a conversation with words like, "Forgive me for my ignorance here, but I don't really know much about ___." Then I'll ask for another's perspective and do my best to listen well. Admitting my ignorance from the get-go frees me to listen without trying to prove I know something.

Holly Daly, a good friend of mine with a long history of seeking racial understanding, points out that another reality White people would do well to accept is that the racial conversation does not have to be fair. Many people approach a conversation with a feeling that things need to be equal, thinking consciously or subconsciously, "If I listen to your experience with racism, then you need to listen to mine and acknowledge that it's equal."[21] This attitude communicates an unwillingness to accept that we've benefitted more because of our skin color than the people of color in our country.

Race relations have never been equal in the U.S., and if White people want to be a healing factor in the equation of racial reconciliation, then we need to know how and when to surrender our own need for 'equality' in order to create places where the painful wounds of inequity have space to breathe, to be heard, and to heal.

Ponder.

1. Do you agree that the racial conversation doesn't need to be 'fair'? Why or why not?
2. Have you ever felt misunderstood by someone? How could they have responded differently to your situation?

Affirm.

While we will never completely understand what it means to walk in another's shoes, we can affirm the reality of other's experiences. What if we simply acknowledged the reality of someone's experience without critique or question or explanation? Phrases like, "I'm so sorry for your pain," or "I can only imagine how that must hurt," go a long way to affirm the experience of someone who feels marginalized. I've also learned to say things like, "Can you help me understand?" or "This doesn't make sense to my White mind. Would you be comfortable telling me how you see it?"

In addition to "I'm listening," the other response Osheta Moore suggests is "I'm sorry." She explains what happens when we use these words:

We're called to be the ones to cry out, "Immeasurable worth!" when image-bearers are devalued. We're the voices of justice. We're the ones who draw in the sand and level the playing field.

As peacemakers, we're tasked with identifying with our Prince of Peace who overcame our blood-thirsty enemy by shedding his own blood—selflessness and love flows from the cross and lies out our chosen path—humility.

"I'm sorry" tames the anger. "I'm sorry" respects the pain. "I'm sorry" positions you as a friend and not adversary.[22]

"But the greatest of these is love."

There's a final tip that I've found the most transformative. It's not so much a tip as it is a magnificent gift because it cannot be forced or created but rather arises organically and unplanned. By far the most life-changing way I've learned to speak of race is under the umbrella of love.

When you love someone, you should naturally do all of the above—*listen, learn, accept, affirm.* When you love someone of a different race, part of the process is listening, learning, accepting, and affirming this part of their experience as well. When we love well, we offer the words *I'm listening* and *I'm sorry* to each other without reservation.

I love and am loved well by so many people of color, and it has changed my world in ways I could have never imagined. As they have spoken their truth out of love for me, I have learned about the fierceness of the human soul, about forgiveness, compassion, and healing in ways I'd never seen in my very-White world. I am deeply indebted to so many who have loved me patiently and consistently across racial lines, for in loving me, they have shown me how to love more deeply. This is, by far, the greatest gift that comes from our relationships.

In the end, while our efforts to grow in racial understanding won't ever be perfect, there is still much we can do to humbly and boldly walk the path toward wholeness and restoration. It's time to stop our pattern of silence by talking, listening, and learning more about our role in the broken racial history of our world. We must intentionally pursue ways in which we can become part of the healing rather than continuing to contribute to the problem.

Ponder.

1. Think of a time when someone affirmed your experience or feelings, even if they did not understand them. What did they say? How did this make you feel?
2. What are ways that you can offer similar affirmations to others?
3. Which phrase is harder for you to say—*I'm listening* or *I'm sorry*? Why?

6

Where to Start W[illegible] Afraid to Talk about Race

Recent headlines overflow with racial turbulence: police violence toward African Americans, racially motivated shootings and protests. Blogger Jamie Wright pins down what I suspect many White people felt about the tragic headlines of the Charleston church shootings:

> *I am afraid to talk about racism for fear of doing it wrong.*
>
> *I'm afraid I'll start a conversation I'm not prepared for, afraid I'll misuse the language of privilege and oppression, afraid I'll offend someone.*
>
> *But I'm not afraid I'll be murdered on the street, or shot at in the park, or slaughtered in a Church for the color of my skin…So it's been easy to stay quiet.*
>
> *To be honest, I still don't know what to say, but I can't keep saying nothing while my neighbor is terrorized by hate and violence. I was born White, but not silent.*
>
> *Racism exists. I won't ignore it.*
>
> *I won't ignore YOU.*[23]

So, what's a Caucasian to do once this admission has been made? How do we move from "I care. I won't ignore this" to actually being part of lasting change? When I ponder this question, conflicting thoughts simmer beneath the surface, leaving me both perplexed and speechless:

> *I have a degree in Multicultural Education, am multilingual, and have taught in communities of color for years. Do I disregard my experiences, my skills, my knowledge because of my privilege?*
>
> *As a teacher, I still hold a position of power within the many communities of color I have known. Do I shun any association of power because of its association with privilege?*
>
> *As a mother, wife, friend, and family member, I walk alongside the daily journey of people of color navigating a world of White privilege. Are these experiences invalidated in the wider world because of the privilege I carry?*
>
> *Having grown up in a predominantly White community and having lived as an adult in many communities of color, I frequently see multiple perspectives of an issue. When do I use my voice and when do I keep quiet?*

These are not easy questions, but they're real ones that churn deep down, rumbling within. I read, talk, and think about race on a regular basis, but there are times when I still feel at a complete loss because of the guilt I carry over my privilege. I know I'm not the only White person who feels this way.

Sometimes, especially when I'm discouraged, it feels like being White disqualifies me from a seat at the racial table. When I whisper this shame-filled admission to those close to me, they respond, "Welcome to my world"—reminding me that not having a seat at the table is no new feeling to people of color.

Ah, privilege. It blinds even those who want to see.

This conversation isn't simple. It's far—both literally and figuratively—from Black and White. So where's a White-person-on-the-sidelines watching all this pain, caring-but-not-experiencing, horrified-and-heartbroken, to start?

As I sit with these questions, I find myself contemplating *who I need to be* in addition to *what I should do* to live in a culturally humble way. The lists of how-to's and to-do's are undeniably helpful, but they'll go nowhere without a fundamental shift in our way of being.

In light of this, I ask myself harder questions than the ones above that reflect my need for self-defense:

- How do I cultivate the type of character that consistently acknowledges my privilege and promotes a good greater than myself?
- Who do I need to become in order to more deeply understand the lives of those who live and think differently than I do?
- How do I seek understanding when I simply do not understand?

- What does love look like toward someone with whom I completely disagree?

The answers that surface are less to-do list, more lifelong goals.

Be ok with messy.

The one firm conclusion I've drawn about race relations is that they are messy. There are valuable points on conflicting sides, endless triggers, and so many speculations on intent.

Could it be true that people of color who have lived in underprivileged communities their entire lives have good reason to not trust the police? *Sure.* Does that mean that all law enforcement officers are racist? *Not exactly.*

Is our society brutal in the way we draw lines between the haves and the have-nots, the ins and the outs? *Definitely, especially when we only use 140 characters to do so.* Do all of our choices exist in a larger social and historical reality of race and power that causes certain people to respond harshly to the story-of-the-day? *For sure.*

Voices from all sides throw 'truth' at each other without acknowledging that sometimes the truth in the realm of people's experience is anything but clear. We operate only within our own skin and this limits our ability to understand each other.

Writer and teacher Heather Plett explains an idea called "holding space" that could close some gaps between these differing cultural realities. She defines *holding space* for another person as a willingness to be present and available in the difficult moments of life. When part of life carries such pain that it's difficult to imagine the next step, those who hold space for others don't judge, try to fix, or make them feel inadequate. Instead, they come alongside and offer warm hearts and open ears.[24]

Parker Palmer calls this idea "the gift of presence" and suggests that giving advice is far more damaging than just walking alongside someone who expresses pain. "The human soul doesn't want to be advised or fixed or saved," he writes. "It simply wants to be witnessed — to be seen, heard and companioned exactly as it is."

He then explains that people who are accustomed to playing the role of "helper" are more concerned with how they are seen than with actually meeting the "soul-deep needs" of others.

> Witnessing and companioning take time and patience, which we often lack—especially when we're in the presence of suffering so painful we can barely stand to be there, as if we were in danger of catching a contagious disease. We want to apply our "fix," then cut and run, figuring we've done the best we can to "save" the other person.[25]

What if "holding space" or offering "the gift of presence" was our sole response to the headlines or to expressions of frustration we might hear from the people of color in our lives? How would the conversation shift if, instead of jumping to immediate conclusions to label sides as right or wrong, we looked first to where we need to 'hold space' for and be present with the brokenness that exists on both sides?

Lean toward pain.

One way I've grown more comfortable with mess is through the practice of walking through pain—both my own and that of others. While it would often feel easier to just close my eyes and turn the other way, digging into the deeper reasons for what causes pain strengthens our ability to understand it. In our broken places, we experience how insincere gestures like offering platitudes or dismissing pain can hurt far more than they help.

Externally, this might look like actively reading on many sides of the headlines or practicing principles offered in this book. Internally, however, it means sitting with a whole lot of uncomfortable. Professor and minister Theresa Latini explains this idea further in her article, *I am a pastor. Here's why I don't want you to pray for me*:

> *Please do not pray for me unless you are willing to walk with me. Know me. Hear the depths of my fear or anguish or whatever it might be and let it affect you.*
>
> *Then let us bring our (not just my) most profound needs vulnerably before God. Please do not try to escape that vulnerability. Because if you do, you have left me, and that*

is not prayer. It is not communion with God through Christ by the spirit.

And if you have no words, that is okay—more than okay, in fact. It's an invitation to sit with me in the awfulness of my predicament and silently wait upon God together.[26]

I would imagine that a whole host of similar prayers are breathed from the mouths of many across America today as we face these racial crises of our day. May it remind us of our need to simply walk alongside and hold space for those in pain today.

Seek first to understand and admit when you don't.

This principle from Stephen Covey's classic, *7 Habits of Highly Effective People*, needs to be revisited in our short-tempered Twitter age. Seeking first to understand means that, rather than constantly throwing out my own opinions, I ask questions and listen to the opinions of others.[27] It means I don't quickly dismiss those with whom I disagree but rather look for ways to understand why they might think that way. It means that I spend time seeking out the perspectives of those with whom I disagree to understand the *what* and *why* of their reasoning.

The hard part about seeking to understand is that sometimes we simply don't. When someone's experience extends beyond our ability to grasp it, we're apt to throw our hands up in frustration and label them idiots. Sometimes, we feel embarrassed by our ignorance so we don't say anything at all.

When I run into a situation involving race that I don't understand, my first response is usually defensive. I like to play devil's advocate, so it's easy for me to dismiss my defensiveness as just being "who I am." However, I've come to recognize that when I grow defensive in race/privilege conversations, it's usually a sign that I need to stop, reflect on what triggered my anger, and revisit the conversation to listen some more. The phrase "help me understand" comes in handy at this point because it focuses my attention on something besides my own (strong) desire to be right and maintain control.

Acknowledge both single and collective stories.

"Stories matter. *Many* stories matter," explains Nigerian author Chimamanda Adichie in her well-known TedTalk, *The Danger of a Single Story*. "Stories have been used to dispossess and to malign, but stories can also be used to empower and to humanize. Stories can break the dignity of a people but stories can also repair that broken dignity."[28]

In contrast to Adichie's perspective, many White Americans are accustomed to telling stories from an individualist perspective. We think about ourselves over the whole, elevating individuals over communities. One way this shows itself in many White churches is their harsher response to individual sins relating to individual sexuality (abortion, pornography, infidelity) than to communal sins like neglect of the poor, consumerism, or gluttony. In contrast, many cultures cultivate a more communal view where individuals consider how their personal actions impact the community as a whole.

In seeking understanding about racial headlines with others, I've learned that I see specific situations through a personal, individual lens. In contrast, others process life through a collective lens that includes painful realities of repeated power and racial abuse through history. Do we both have valid points? Yes, we're just processing through different lenses.

Create space to listen.

The breakneck speed of our culture robs us from time to consider both our place in the world and our impact on those around us. Contrary to the story of the freeways, we are not meant to live at break-neck speed every minute of the day. Unless we build barriers around and stoplights into our lives, we might hurtle ourselves right over the edge without even noticing.

For our roots to grow deep, we must create space to attend to all the realities of life, not just the easiest ones. Finding spaces to pause and sort through our thoughts, feelings, and experiences is crucial if we want to incorporate any of the above goals effectively. Pausing looks different for everyone. Some people listen to podcasts or sermons that inspire. Others retreat to nature and quiet space. Some prefer to write, read, or chat over coffee with a friend. Whatever the method, intentionally creating space to allow ourselves to reflect deeply and sit with discomfort is key to long-term and sustained internal change.

Socrates challenged, "Let him that would move the world first move himself." May his timeless words charge us to move ourselves before we move the world and remind us of the need to act beyond the horror of the headlines by starting with the one thing we all have the power to change: ourselves.

Don't over-spiritualize racism.

In the children's classic *Roll of Thunder, Hear My Cry,* an African American mother attempts to explain the harshness of 1930s Southern racism to her young daughter, Cassie. After offering a brief history of slavery, she describes the historical relationship between White Christian slave owners and African American slaves:

> *"They also said that slavery was good for us because it taught us to be good Christians—like the White people... But they didn't teach us Christianity to save our souls, but to teach us obedience. They were afraid of slave revolts and they wanted us to learn the Bible's teachings about slaves being loyal to their masters."*[29]

It saddens me to think of how slowly some things change. When race comes up in conversations among White Christians, it's not uncommon to hear responses along these lines:

> *"This isn't a* race *issue. It's a* sin *issue."*

> *"We all belong to one family in Christ. Why can't we just all get along?"*

> *"We need to be focusing on unity. The topic of racism is too divisive."*

While these responses aren't exactly what Cassie's mama encountered from the White-Folk almost a century ago, they still carry whispers of the same sentiments. When we make the above statements, history reinforces that they're likely to make a wildly different impact than their original intent:

> *"Quit giving us a hard time. We're not bad people."*

> *"It only matters to me that I feel comfortable. If you have a problem, you need to keep it to yourself."*

> *"Unity is about conforming to the majority. If you don't fit the majority, you don't matter."*

It hurts, I know.

But let's press pause on the "unity" button for just a minute. We need to do some sustained reflection on the causes of the "disunity" first.

Thankfully, overt racism is no longer legally acceptable in society. What makes this change especially challenging, though, is that it leaves White people with the impression that racism no longer exists. As a result, many White Christians begin the race conversation by dismissing racial pain with the hammer of spiritual language. Throwing Bible verses to cover up the realities of racism is essentially the Christianized version of "Shut-the-%$#&-up. I don't want to hear what you have to say."

When the history of race relations in our country includes stories of Christian White people converting Blacks for the purpose of subservience, Japanese-American internment, and Native American genocide, it's essential to be very, very careful not to use spiritual language to silence pleas to be heard.

So, what do we do instead?

A Bible verse doesn't become Christian until it's actually *lived out*. It's the *living* of these verses that creates deep change, not merely the *speaking* of them. Philippians 2 again provides an excellent model of humility for White people engaging the race conversation. Let's consider what this language might look like in everyday actions:

- ***Be tender and compassionate*** = Listen to, learn from, accept, and affirm the shared experiences of people of color. Mourn over the challenges they express and listen closely to the reasons behind their pain.
- ***Do nothing out of selfish ambition or vain conceit*** = Seek to understand the realities of a racially privileged system without worrying about feeling 'blamed'. Sometimes White people get stuck in the conversation because "my family didn't own slaves." That's not the point—acknowledging the bigger picture of systemic injustice is.
- ***Value others above yourselves*** = Fill your lives with their stories. Watch movies on the civil rights movement. Read books about its leaders. Move out of comfort zones into a

place that feels unsettling. Pause to consider what life might look like through someone else's eyes.

- ***Don't consider equality something to be used to your own advantage*** = Look for ways to pursue equity (fairness) over equality (sameness)[30] so that all people might have better access to privileges the majority holds. Learn more about concepts like *White privilege* and *cultural appropriation* as a means of valuing and respecting others.
- ***Take on the humble nature of a servant*** = Listen, listen, listen, listen, and then listen some more. When we speak before we understand, too many words grow heavy in the hearts of those with whom we share. Find ways to learn about the perplexing parts of race relations that fatigue people of color who have borne the weight of the ignorance of the majority for centuries.

All of these are helpful steps toward meaningful racial reconciliation, but, for the (literal) love of God, please stop silencing the voices of people of color through the flippant use of Christian words. It doesn't cultivate change. It merely silences long-ignored voices, fosters anger, and destroys the very peace Jesus came to bring.

Ponder.

1. Which of these goals sounds most difficult for you? What is a practical step you could take to pursue that goal?

2. Which of these skills have you utilized in other areas of your life? How might this experience help you better understand race relations?

3. Think of a "spiritualized phrase" you frequently use. Brainstorm a way to express this sentiment using everyday—not Christian—language. Reflect on how you would feel if someone said these words in a challenging situation.

7

Dealing with Anger in Race Relations

One of the most difficult reasons it can be hard to talk about race is because of the anger that often comes up in such conversations. This, too, is a facet of this issue that White people must seek to understand more deeply.

My first teaching job was in an historic Black school in a Midwestern city, and it was a crash course in understanding the dynamics of urban settings, race, and poverty. Being brand new to the professional world, it is highly probable that my youthfulness translated into a White-savioresque attitude à la *Dangerous Minds*, even though I didn't consciously enter with this perspective. In spite of my intentions, I encountered two quite contrasting responses to my naïveté.

The first was from an African American teacher next door who railed angrily at me one day for something I'd done that irked her. I don't remember a word of what she actually said to me, but I clearly remember returning to my classroom in tears, feeling crushed by her anger and assumptions regarding my White ignorance. I'd tried to seek her insight out on previous (failed) attempts, and now she'd shut me down for good. From that point on, our relationship was one of icy glares and cold shoulders.

The other response was from another African American teacher who kindly took me under her wing. She showered me with hugs as she gently taught me the basics of African American history and urban culture. She took kids home with her when they needed a mama and brought them breakfast at school when they were hungry. All the kids knew that you went to her classroom first if you needed some extra love, and I followed their lead frequently.

While Loving Teacher's response felt better than Angry Teacher's harshness toward me, both reactions taught me vital lessons in the world of race relations. Nearly twenty years later, I cringe at my youthful self with a grateful nod to the lesson Angry Teacher taught me. After I got past the initial sting of the Angry Teacher's reaction (which, I might sheepishly add, took years), I began to contemplate why she may have responded the way she did. She'd lived down the street from these kids and their parents and their pastors for longer than I'd been alive, and she knew a reality that I did not.

As I've reflected on it over the years, I'd guess that her anger stemmed more from the continued systemic racial injustice that she navigated daily rather than from my specific actions. My young White naiveté and curiosity simply represented the cycle of systemic injustice that had wreaked havoc on her home, and it (understandably) made her angry with me. For all the good I hoped to do in that context, it forced me to acknowledge that she was the one with the lasting influence and that I was simply an observer passing through.

I have often heard people of color express a similar anger toward the inequitable system that keeps racism alive and kicking, but living with my non-White family in a majority White setting made my experience with anger and race take a whole new turn. The longer we lived in a white community, the harder it was for me to assume good-intentions when the bad actions were so obvious. Over time, I grew angry with White people myself.

I was angry that 'my people' wouldn't embrace my family like they did people who fit into their pretty-little-cornfield-box. I was angry they didn't care enough about the outside world to understand people from it. I was angry they clammed up and smiled when they didn't understand something rather than just admit it outright. I was angry they dismissed others' perspectives with Christian platitudes just to keep the peace.

Over the years, I've asked people I hold in great esteem how they've managed to keep going through the anger that inevitably comes with interracial relationships. I've had more than one ~~day~~ year when I've shut down on the whole thing. The last bout in the cornfields nearly did me in completely; but then, the air came as we surfaced somewhere near Los Angeles, gasping for breath. We sat quietly recovering in the shadow of the mountains and on the edge of the sea for over a year.

Little by little, I sorted out the pieces of my anger over our experience in a land that did not understand its impact on those who were different within its borders. Since everyone processes these things differently, I'll recap a few things I learned about processing racial anger along the way.

It's ok to be angry.

The polite Christian Midwesterner in me would disagree with this statement, but I've learned that denying anger only makes it sink deeper. Bringing it to light it at an appropriate time and place helps to shed light on what's my responsibility and what's not.

In the process of walking with my anger, I'm also learning to distinguish between a productive anger that produces fruit and an explosive anger that spews ickiness over everyone. As a person from an emotionally reserved culture, however, I've also had to accept that it *is* ok to share pain and anger in the right place and at the right time.

Expressing anger is both cultural and individual.

Personally, I rarely yell or scream when I'm angry. Instead, I grow very quiet. This happens to work well in my home culture where many shut down and numb out in response to screaming and yelling. You can imagine my shock, however, to encounter people who 'yelled' at each other only to start a hug-fest and productive conversation a few moments later.

Everyone subscribes to unspoken personal and cultural rules regarding the expression of anger, but few of us follow the same ones. Letting go of my need to apply my internal rules to the rest of the world helps me to listen better when I encounter an anger expressed differently from my own.

Jesus is not a band-aid.

It's human nature to want a quick fix, but also equally human for that fix to be complex and layered. Sticking Jesus on the massive wound of racial and systemic injustice doesn't heal anything, it only makes Jesus look inadequate and small.

While I'm a firm believer that walking with Jesus in our moments can give us the ability to walk alongside one another's pain or anger, it's not the same as understanding others' stories by listening to them with our ears, our hearts, and our lives. To say that 'the only solution is Jesus' and that angry voices should just 'pray about it' implies that we don't need to do anything but piously bow our heads, open our Bibles, and sing songs for everything to get better.

In reality, there is no quick fix. The journey of reconciliation is a long, slow walk in which spiritual platitudes become roadblocks and polite smiles translate into yield signs.

Injustice is painful.

I've occasionally caught myself whining, "Why me?" in response to difficulties, but when I live in light of a global reality, I find that the more appropriate question is, "Why not me?" What better lesson for the middle-class-White-girl-with-an-education to learn? My privilege sneaks up on me so subtly that I hardly notice it, and coming face-to-face with injustice gives me a stark reality check on what the majority of the world faces every day. The more quickly I accept this pain, the more humbly I learn to walk in it.

Forgiveness takes time.

A former African American pastor of mine recommended that I walk in the way of Jesus by following His words, "Father, forgive them, for they know not what they do"—even when 'they' likely know what they're doing because that *still* shows a better way.[31] Another guide gave me permission to take time away to be imperfect and angry for a while. When people hold those you love at arms' length, it hurts, and I needed some private time and space to grieve this reality.

Savor the good moments.

While the overarching flavor of our racial and cultural isolation was bitter, there were all sorts of sweet-and-holy moments and plenty of individual people who, in spite of the prevailing environment, embraced us open-armed in their homes and their hearts. Pausing to sit with these gentle memories softens the anger and refocuses me toward grace and goodness.

These days, when I sit with a person of color, listening to them express the conflict of being the only one, wondering if they were chosen for their skill or their skin color, or grieving over the incredulous ignorance of a White leader's words, what I hear first is pain, even when it sounds like anger. I hear sadness over what hasn't changed and grief over the White majority's lack of understanding of their inherent privilege and power. I hear weariness over walking the same path time and again, wondering if change will ever happen, if the majority will ever really care enough to understand.

I am, however, only one small voice and two small ears. What I say and hear is only a piece of the story. Like Loving Teacher and Angry Teacher, everyone processes the brokenness of our racial history differently, and each voice tells a story we need to hear—even the angry ones.

Speak from your scars, not your wounds.[32]

One of the reasons the race conversation in America today remains explosive is because people are speaking from fresh wounds instead of healed scars. Because of the long-lasting impact of systems established to privilege white people and disadvantage other races, racism is not a thing of the past but a stark reality of the present. When we hear angry voices—or use them ourselves—what we really hear are the festering wounds of this reality.

When a wound is fresh, it is tender and delicate. We move carefully, protecting it from additional harm or further damage. If someone approaches it carelessly, it's instinctive to lash out in an effort to keep the wounded area safe. When I found myself freshly wounded by the impact of racism on my family, the tenderness led me to quiet spaces and safe friends who I knew would hold us gently while we healed. There were days when I felt as though we might take cover forever in the grand cultural patchwork of Los Angeles, leaving the white community in our distant past. As time healed those wounds, however, my heart moved toward healing one word at a time. I realized that hiding from my whiteness and its impact on those around me is an action reflecting my woundedness, not my healing.

While the scars remain, the wounds no longer gape. In fact, as I speak from my scars, I find a strength within them born from the painful process of healing. If only more of Christ's followers would understand the same from this broken racial road we walk—that when we admit weakness to one another, seek forgiveness, and walk toward each another in humility, Christ's kingdom grows stronger, and so do we.

Ponder.

1. Have you ever experienced racial anger (either yours or someone else's)? Reflect on how you responded to the anger.
2. How do you handle anger in general? Do you implode, explode, or avoid? How does your response affect your ability to understand the issues that cause the anger?
3. Do you speak from your wounds or your scars? What is the impact of this on yourself and those around you?

Epilogue

The Charge

I'm Jody, and I'm a White person.

This is not my only identity, but it is certainly a piece of it. The more I understand how it shapes me and, in turn, how this affects those around me, the more I will become a peacemaker rather than a conflict instigator.

Will you join me?

The road is long and the journey a bit bumpy at times, but the destination is one of vulnerability, hope, and restoration. Let us not shut our eyes, our hearts, or our mouths, but rather open them to those around us, creating space for everyone in our midst, not only those just like ourselves.

With gentle steps and hopeful hearts, may this be our ever-present prayer:

> ***Give us awareness*** *to let down our guard and lean into the fear that keeps us silent in conversations about race.*
>
> ***Give us courage to face our guilt*** *by learning how our cultural values shape our internal definitions of what is valuable.*
>
> ***Give us strength to face the brokenness of our history*** *and speak with the purpose of creating healing.*

Give us a desire to increase our understanding *by listening to and learning from the voices of those whose stories and whose access to power differ from ours.*

Help us acknowledge our propensity to hold tight to power *by loosening our grip and looking always to understand before we are understood.*

Keep us from accusing or defending, *and teach us to respond with humility and compassion, especially when we don't agree or understand.*

Make us, Lord, like you—*humble servants who value others more than themselves. Show us our conceit so that we might bring reconciliation and peace to your body.*

Amen. Come, Lord Jesus. Come.

Appendix A

Movies and Documentaries about Race

Beware of the Hollywood machine as you watch movies about race. It loves to tell White savior stories on the big screen. When the only stories we see are ones of White people helping poor Black people, our subconscious sense of superiority is reinforced. Some popular movies that reinforce this story are:

- Dangerous Minds (1995)
- The Help (2011)
- Dances with Wolves (1990)
- Freedom Writers (2007)
- The Blind Side (2009)

While many of these movies tell great stories, they don't tell the *only* stories. It's important to also gain an understanding of the inherent strength and dignity that belong to all people apart from the dominant White story. Some great movies/documentaries that tell these stories are:

- African American Lives (2006)
- The Butler (2013)
- Central Park 5 (2013)
- Claudine (1974)
- Crash (2004)
- Fruitvale Station (2013)
- The Learning Tree (1969)
- Twelve Years a Slave (2013)

Appendix B

Recommended Reading

Articles

All article titles are easily located through an internet search.

I Like Your Christ, I Do Not Like Your Christian Language by Cindy Brandt

Privilege Says... by Christena Cleveland

Explaining White Privilege to a Broke Person by Gina Crossley-Corcoran

In the Face of Hate—Love out Loud by Marilyn Gardner

To the (probably White) Person who Says it Shouldn't Be about Race by Jelani Greenidge

An Open Letter to the Evangelical Church: I am not Your Punchline by Kathy Khang

White Privilege: Unpacking the Invisible Knapsack by Peggy McIntosh

Gate A-4 by Naomi Shihab Nye

Hidden Assumptions and Minorities' Burdens by Sam Tseng

How Going on Vacation Might be Better than Going on a Mission by Jamie Wright

The Asian American Awakening: That Moment You Realize You're Not White by Connie Zhou

Books

Disunity in Christ: Uncovering the Hidden Forces that Keep us Apart by Christena Cleveland

More than Serving Tea: Asian American Women on Expectations, Relationships, Leadership and Faith by Asifa Dean, Chistie Heller de Leon, Kathy Khang, Nikki Toyama-Szeto, Tracey Gee, and Jeanette Yep

Divided by Faith: Evangelical Religion and the Problem of Race in American by Michael O. Emerson and Christian Smith

Reconciliation Blues: A Black Evangelical's View Inside View of White Christianity by Edward Gilbreath

Theirs is the Kingdom: Celebrating the Gospel in Urban America by Robert D. Lupton

Let Justice Roll Down by John Perkins

The Next Evangelicalism: Freeing the Church from Western Cultural Captivity by Soong Chan Rah

Being White: Finding our Place in a Multiethnic World by Paula Harris and Doug Schaupp

Welcoming the Stranger: Justice, Compassion & Truth in the Immigration Debate by Matthew Soerens and Jenny Hwang Yang

Why do all the Black Kids Sit Together in the Cafeteria by Beverly Daniels Tatum

Silent Racism: How Well-Meaning White People Perpetuate the Racial Divide by Barbara Trepagnier

Race Matters by Cornel West

Appendix C

21 Day Race Challenge

21 days toward a deeper understanding of race relations
All articles / terms are easily located through an internet search

1. Read Peggy McIntosh's article "White Privilege: Unpacking the Invisible Knapsack."
2. Watch "A Look at Race Relations through a child's eyes" on YouTube.
3. Learn more about racial microagressions.
4. Watch an episode of Henry Louis Gates, Jr.'s documentary "African American Lives" on PBS.com.
5. Learn more about being the only one. Read "The Onlies" on Austin Channing's website (austinchanning.com).
6. Read "Privilege says…" on Christena Cleveland's website (christenacleveland.com).
7. Watch Brian Stevenson's TedTalk, "We need to talk about injustice."
8. Choose an ethnic recipe and purchase the ingredients in an ethnic grocery store. Linger as you shop and notice your surroundings.
9. Reflect on your own cultural heritage using "The Iceberg Concept of Culture"
10. Read Eugene Cho's article, "Thanksgiving and Genocide: Let's write and share a more honest story."
11. Watch a video about immigration on G92.org/watch.
12. Visit a church of a different ethnic group.

13. Read Christena Cleveland's article, "Everything I need to know about racism I learned from the church."
14. Watch "Dr. Cornel West tells us about race, values, and lives worth living" on YouTube.
15. Read "The Names They Gave Me" by Tasbeeh Herwees.
16. Consider the implications of a White Jesus in Jonathan Merritt's article, "Insisting Jesus was White is bad history and bad theology" or in Christena Cleveland's article "Why Jesus' skin color matters".
17. Reflect on the impact of racial jokes with Kathy Khang in her article, "An open letter to the evangelical church: I am not your punchline."
18. Watch Christena Cleveland speak about "Does Christianity make people prejudiced?" on qideas.org.
19. Watch Michelle Higgins' speech on #BlackLivesMatter from the Urbana 2015 conference.
20. Learn about a child's cultural experience being validated in Mitali Perkin's story, "The Magic Carpet."
21. Take an implicit bias quiz on ProjectImplicit.

You may also access a clickable, hyper-linked version of many of these resources at: https://thelinkbetween.files.wordpress.com/2014/02/30-day-race-challenge.pdf

Endnotes

[1] Bailey, S.P. (2013, Sept 13). *Rick Warren gets backlash from Asian American Christians for posting photo.* Retrieved from http://religionnews.com/2013/09/25/rick-warren-gets-backlash-asian-american-christians-posting-photo/

[2] Passion [PassionVevo]. (2013, April 12). *How great is our God (World Edition)* [video file]. Retrieved from https://www.youtube.com/watch?v=vg5qDljEw7Q.

[3] Fortgang, T. (2014, April 30). *Checking my privilege: Character as the basis of privilege.* Retrieved from http://www.realclearpolitics.com/articles/2014/04/30/checking_my_privilege_character_as_the_basis_of_privilege_122473.html

[4] Brown, B. (2010). *The gifts of imperfection: let go of who you think you're supposed to be and embrace who you are.* Center City, Minnesota: Hazelden.

[5] Brown, A. C. (2014). *Unlearning.* Retrieved from http://austinchanning.com/blog/2014/4/unlearning

[6] McIntosh, P. (2009). White people facing race: Uncovering the myths that keep racism in place. Retrieved from http://mntheateralliance.org/docs/wic/WIC_White_People_Facing_Race.pdf

[7] Tatum, B. (1997). *Why are all the black kids sitting together in the cafeteria.* New York, NY: Baker Books.

[8] Ibid.

[9] Breslow, J., Wexler, E., & Collins, R. (2014). The return of school segregation in eight charts. Retrieved from http://www.pbs.org/wgbh/frontline/article/the-return-of-school-segregation-in-eight-charts/.

[10] Grant, B. (2003). *What is gentrification?* Retrieved from http://www.pbs.org/pov/flagwars/what-is-gentrification/.

[11] Gilbreath, Edward. (2006). Reconciliation blues: A black evangelical's inside view of White Christianity. Madison, WI: Intervarsity Press.

[12] Ibid.

[13] Howard, G. (2006). *We can't teach what we don't know: White teachers, multiracial schools.* New York, NY: Teachers Press.

[14] Cleveland, Christena. (2013). *Disunity in Christ: Uncovering the hidden forces that keep us apart.* Madison, WI: Intervarsity Press.

[15] Tatum, B. (1997). *Why are all the black kids sitting together in the cafeteria.* New York, NY: Baker Books.

[16] Ibid.

[17] Pipher, M.B. (2002). *The middle of everywhere: The world's refugees come to our town.* New York: Harcourt.

[18] Visser, S. (2014, January 15). Online communication.

[19] Moore, O. (2015, June 18). *What I need you to say in response to the Charleston shooting.* Retrieved from https://oshetablogs.wordpress.com/2015/06/18/what-i-need-you-say-in-response-to-the-shooting-in-charleston/

[20] Smith, W. (2007). Assume the position...You fit the description. Psychosocial experiences and racial battle fatigue among African American male college students. *American Behavioral Scientist 51*(4), 251-278.

[21] Daly, H. (2014, January 15). Online communication.

[22] Moore, O. (2015, June 18). *What I need you to say in response to the Charleston shooting.* Retrieved from https://oshetablogs.wordpress.com/2015/06/18/what-i-need-you-say-in-response-to-the-shooting-in-charleston/

[23] Wright, J. (2015, June 18). I am afraid to talk about racism for fear of doing it wrong. [Facebook status update]. Retrieved from https://www.facebook.com/jamietheveryworstmissionary/posts/835599949840537.

[24] Plett, L. (2015). *What it means to hold space for people, plus eight tips on how to do it well.* Retrieved from http://heatherplett.com/2015/03/hold-space/

[25] Palmer, P. (2016). *The gift of presence. The perils of advice.* Retrieved from http://www.onbeing.org/blog/parker-palmer-the-gift-of-presence-the-perils-of-advice/8628

[26] Latini, T. (2015). *I am a pastor. Here's why I don't want you to pray for me.* Retrieved from http://www.washingtonpost.com/news/acts-of-faith/wp/2015/05/07/i-am-a-pastor-heres-why-i-dont-want-you-to-pray-for-me/

[27] Covey, S. R. (2005). *The 7 habits of highly effective people*. London: Simon & Schuster.

[28] Adichie, C. [Ted]. (2009, October 7). *The danger of a single story* [video file]. Retrieved from https://www.youtube.com/watch?t=1&v=D9Ihs241zeg

[29] Taylor, M.D. (1976). *Roll of thunder, hear my cry. New York: Dial Press.*

[30] Office of Equity and Human Rights. (n.d.). The problem with "equality". Retrieved from https://www.portlandoregon.gov/oehr/article/449547

[31] Edwards, D. (2013, May 23). Online communication.

[32] Smith, S. [heystephsmith]. (2016, April 16). "I try to preach from my scars, not my wounds." -@Sarcasticluther [Tweet]. Retrieved from https://twitter.com/heystephsmith/status/721490932365987840